Air
Is Everywhere

by Megan McDonald

What You Already Know

Matter is all around you. Matter is anything that takes up space and has mass. Everything that has matter has mass. Mass is the amount of matter in an object. Different kinds of matter have different properties. A property is something about an object that you can observe with your senses. For example, the color and shape of an object are its properties.

There are three different states of matter. Matter can be a solid, liquid, or gas. A solid is matter that has its own size and shape. Solids take up space and have mass. Liquid is matter that does not have its own shape. Liquids take the shape of their containers. Liquids take up space and have mass. Gas is matter that takes the size and shape of its container. Gas has mass.

Matter can be changed in different ways. You can change the size or shape of matter. You can also stir matter together to make a mixture. A mixture is something made up of two or more things that do not change. You can separate a mixture and see each part.

Another way to change matter is by cooling or heating it. Water is matter. You can cool water enough to turn it into ice. You can heat the ice to turn it back into liquid. You can even heat liquid water enough to turn it into gas. The water evaporates into the air.

You are about to read more about one state of matter. Air is a gas, and it is all around us.

What is air?

Air is a gas. It is all around us. Air is made up of tiny particles called molecules. We cannot see air molecules, but they take up space and have mass.

Air is touching us all the time. We cannot see air, but sometimes we can feel it. Have you ever felt the wind on your skin? That is air.

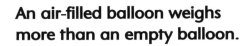

An air-filled balloon weighs more than an empty balloon.

We can also see what air does around us. The wind can carry a kite. It can make trees sway. When you blow up a balloon, you are filling it with air. Now the balloon takes up more space and weighs more.

Air for Life

Air is important for life. Air contains oxygen. We need oxygen to breathe. Oxygen in the air helps our bodies release energy from the food we eat. The more active we are, the more oxygen we need. People need to take in a lot of air when they play sports.

Astronauts bring air with them to space.

Air is thinner up high. This means that there are fewer air molecules. If you climb a tall mountain, you will need to breathe faster. This happens because it is harder for you to get the air you need.

In space, there is no air at all. This is why astronauts must carry air with them. They breathe air from special tanks on their backs.

Air and Plants

Plants need air too. They use air to get energy from their food. Plants use different gases found in the air.

One of the gases they use is carbon dioxide. Plants use carbon dioxide, water, and sunlight to make food in their leaves. This is called photosynthesis.

Many plants also need air for another reason. The wind helps spread their seeds. Some plants, such as dandelions, have seeds that are connected to fluff. The wind carries the fluff through the air. When the wind stops blowing, the seeds fall to the ground. Then new plants can grow.

These seeds get scattered by air.

Air on the Move

Air moves all the time. Moving air is called wind. Wind is caused by different temperatures of air. Warmer, lighter air gets pushed along by cooler, heavier air. Sometimes wind can be a soft, light breeze. Sometimes it can be strong, such as a hurricane or a tornado.

Hurricanes are storms with powerful winds. The center of a hurricane is called the hurricane's eye. The eye of a hurricane is calm. The winds around the eye are very strong. Hurricanes have winds that move more than one hundred miles per hour.

Tornadoes are twisting winds that form a funnel-shaped cloud. When this touches down, it tears up everything in its path. The winds of a tornado can reach a speed of three hundred miles per hour.

Tornadoes can be very dangerous.

Wind Power

Wind is very powerful. Sometimes, as with hurricanes and tornadoes, wind can be dangerous. Sometimes we can use the power of the wind to help us. Windmills capture energy from the wind. This energy can then be used in many ways.

People have been using windmills for centuries.

The wind blows on the blades of the windmill and spins them like a pinwheel. The turning blades, or vanes, can run machines.

People have been using windmills for hundreds of years to pump water and grind grain. Today, people use wind power to make electricity. The energy that moves through wind turbines could power whole cities.

Rising Air

Hot air is lighter than cool air. Air that is warm rises up. People can use hang gliders to soar through the air. Birds, such as eagles and sea gulls, soar on rising waves of air. The warm air keeps the birds' bodies lifted. Birds that glide have big wings so they can catch as much air as possible.

An eagle rides on a wave of warm air.

Hot air balloons make use of warm, rising air.

 A hot air balloon can float because it has warm air in it. The bag of air is heated by a burner under the balloon. The balloon rises until the temperature of the air inside the bag is the same as the air outside. As the air in the bag cools, the balloon slowly starts to go down. The people inside can control the balloon by warming or cooling the air.

Moisture in the Air

Air has moisture in it. This moisture is called water vapor. Water vapor is a gas. Warm air and water vapor rise. Then they cool. When air cools, the water vapor in it condenses to form clouds. Moisture from clouds is frozen when it begins to fall. If the air is warm, it changes to rain.

Rain and snow are kinds of precipitation.

When the clouds become heavy enough, the water falls to the ground as rain. Scientists call this precipitation.

Snow is another kind of precipitation. Water droplets in clouds turn into snowflakes when the air is below freezing. Snow has a lot of air trapped in it. This is why snow looks white.

Air Resistance

Air resistance is a force that slows down objects moving through air. You can feel air resistance when you go down a hill on your bike. It feels like the air is pushing against you.

Air resistance helps these parachutes fall gently to the ground.

Air resistance helps people land parachutes. It slows them down as they fall through the air. Parachutes are big pieces of cloth. They are made to catch a lot of air resistance.

Air resistance can be a problem. People do not want cars and planes to be slowed down by air. Cars and planes have special shapes so they get less air resistance.

Air Under Pressure

Tiny molecules of air that we cannot see press down on objects around them. This is called air pressure. Air molecules can cause pressure because they take up space and have weight.

Air pressure gets less strong the higher we go, because there are fewer air molecules. We are so used to the air pushing against us that we do not even feel it!

The air in these bicycle tires is under pressure.

Air is springy. It pushes back when you squash it. If you squeeze air into a small space, the tiny air molecules get pushed together. The air pressure in that space gets stronger.

You can feel the pressure of air when you squeeze a ball or a bicycle tire. The air is pushed into a smaller space and feels tight. When you let go, the ball or tire will spring out again. The air molecules have pushed back.

Some machines work using high-pressure air. Some drills can even use air pressure to blast holes in concrete.

This drill uses the strong force of air under pressure.

Air Is Important

Air is an important gas. Without air, we could not live. People need oxygen in the air to breathe and to get energy. Plants use carbon dioxide in the air to make their food.

Air heats up, moves, rises, and cools. It helps create clouds, rain, and wind. Some winds, such as tornadoes, can be dangerous. Wind can also be very useful. Wind can scatter seeds from plants. It can power windmills.

People use air for fun too. Hot air balloons use air to float up into the sky. Windsurfers use the wind to dart across the water. Airplanes speed through the air to bring people to faraway places.

Air is necessary for life. It is useful and fun. Look around you. Feel it on your skin. Air is everywhere.

Glossary

air pressure the pushing force made by the weight of tiny molecules of air

air resistance the force of air slowing down objects moving through it

condenses changes from water vapor to liquid water

evaporates changes from a liquid into a gas

molecules tiny, invisible particles that make up matter

photosynthesis the process through which green plants make food in their leaves

precipitation water that falls to the ground as rain, snow, or hail

What did you learn?

1. What state of matter is air?

2. What is photosynthesis?

3. **Writing** in Science Air is important to life. Write to describe three ways in which air helps us live. Use words from the book as you write.

4. **Draw Conclusions** Why is it important for the wind to spread seeds?

Genre	Comprehension Skill	Text Features	Science Content
Nonfiction	Draw Conclusions	• Captions • Glossary	Matter

Scott Foresman Science 2.8

PEARSON

Scott Foresman

scottforesman.com

How Do Boats Float?

by Nairobi Toller

Vocabulary

atom
buoyancy
density
element
mass
matter
periodic table
pressure
property
volume

Extended Vocabulary

balsa wood
cargo ship
displace
hull
steel
swim bladder
withstand

Picture Credits

Every effort has been made to secure permission and provide appropriate credit for photographic material.
The publisher deeply regrets any omission and pledges to correct errors called to its attention in subsequent editions.

Photo locators denoted as follows: Top (T), Center (C), Bottom (B), Left (L), Right (R), Background (Bkgd).

Opener: Lester Lefkowitz/Corbis ; 1 Doug Wilson/Corbis; 5 Doug Wilson/Corbis; 9 (BR) ©SPL/Photo Researchers, Inc.;
10 Lester Lefkowitz/Corbis.

Scott Foresman/Dorling Kindersley would also like to thank: 15 (CA) IFREMER, Paris/DK Images.

Unless otherwise acknowledged, all photographs are the copyright © of Dorling Kindersley, a division of Pearson.

ISBN: 0-328-13837-1

3 4 5 6 7 8 9 10 V010 13 12 11 10 09 08 07 06 05